Dedicated to Black folks
living their best lives
wherever they may be

Black in Asia

Preface

My name is Tiffany Huang and I am the founder of Spill Stories, a storytelling platform uniting womxn of color around the world. I am proud to share this anthology of 23 stories from Black writers who have lived across South Korea, Hong Kong, Japan, Taiwan, China, Thailand, Singapore, Vietnam, Myanmar, and Mongolia. These stories were first featured on our Instagram (@spillstories), which features prose and poetry around social topics that provide catharsis for the readers and writers alike. Since 2018, Spill Stories has shared stories online and curated offline community events such as book launches, spoken word events, and writing workshops.

In March 2020, we completed a virtual writers workshop during the height of Covid-19 in Asia. The workshop was brilliantly facilitated by Boipelo Seswane (@bopzybee), a South African writer and teacher based in Seoul. Several of the writers in this book from Hong Kong and Seoul attended that workshop via video conference. We compiled around six stories at that time.

A few months later, George Floyd was brutally murdered by the police. In response, the Black Lives Matter movement spread across the world to bring justice, healing, and freedom to Black people across the globe. To amplify Black voices, we started publishing some of the stories from the workshop. After a few stories were published, an influx of other writers wanted to share their stories. The series only grew from there.

These stories are really special to me because they broaden the conversation about the Black Lives Matter movement beyond the United States. As a Taiwanese American ally, I had a few conversations with non-Black friends about the Black Lives Matter movement. They consistently responded that the movement was relevant for the States and Europe, but it wasn't needed in Asia. I asked them why, and they said there simply were not that many Black people in Asia, and there were bigger issues to care about, like income inequality, government surveillance, or economic recession, depending on the country. One person went as far as to say that discussing race in Asia was a matter of privilege and out of touch with daily struggles of the working class.

It is true that Black people in most Asian countries do not make up as high of a percentage of the population compared to Black people in the States, which stands at around 13 percent. However, to use that statistic as rationale to claim that racism is not an issue in Asia is an ambitious act of mental gymnastics. While the framework of race relations in the US cannot be copied and pasted for the rest of the world due to different histories and cultures, racism is endemic in Asia. I fervently believe that racism is so pervasive across the continent today that it is oftentimes unnoticed, accepted, or, at worst, encouraged, rather than discussed and deconstructed.

In order to understand racism in Asia, it is helpful to remind ourselves that race is a social construct, and there is no objective classification of people by color. The common racial groups that are usually applied in the States are not the best lens to understand racism here. In Asia, discrimination is not only about one color versus another; it is much more nuanced. Some Chinese people still exhibit resentment towards Japanese people due to WWII. Southeast Asians are discriminated in Hong Kong as 'lesser-than'. Colorism is rampant within most, if not all, countries, with lighter-skinned people deemed as most attractive. The perceptions among East, Southeast, and South Asians is fraught with stereotypes. In Asia, there is plenty of discrimination to be discussed before even leaving the continent, and then there is another conversation about racism towards people outside of it. In totality, discrimination and racism here is the messy confluence of appearance, history, and culture, like a very complicated spider web.

These perceptions, passed down generations, come from a multitude of concepts, like colonialism, war, nationalism, ethnic homogeneity across countries, etc. I'll acknowledge colonialism and ethnic homogeneity, although the following paragraphs won't do the topics justice. The majority of countries in Asia have been colonized by the West, which has come hand in hand with white supremacy, racial and ethnic discrimination, and social hierarchies based on factors such as color and language abilities. The aftermath of colonialism led to the unequal distribution of resources, with white colonists as the primary beneficiaries. Indigenous and migrant populations were hit the hardest in regards to loss of land, inaccessibility of higher education, lack of public welfare programs, and exploited labor. Colonialism's aftermath has perpetuated the very economic inequalities that people deem "more important" than racism.

The homogeneity of many Asian countries (with Northeast Asian countries being the least diverse) also means that people of the dominant ethnic groups in each country are not regularly exposed to others who do not look like them. National identity, therefore, is a matter of appearance, rather than lived cultural experience in many Asian countries. The effects of appearance-based identity are endless and of differing severity on people's livelihoods. Biracial people are often not accepted in their home countries until they win an Olympic medal (e.g., Naomi Osaka). Ethnic minorities are subject to being monitored and stopped by the police to be asked about their immigration status. In 2019, Thailand's Prime Minister defended police for requesting information about minority Muslim students from universities around the country. This April, Chinese authorities in Guangzhou, which has China's largest African community, began a campaign to forcibly test Africans for Covid-19 and evict them from their homes.

In a great show of irony, I was lucky enough to visit the Taj Mahal in January this year. My tour guide insisted that Rohingya Muslims were not truly Indian because they were Muslim immigrants from another country, and therefore did not deserve to stay in India. I asked him if he found his own words contradictory, because his vocation was dedicated to celebrating a monument created by the Mughal empire, which practiced Islam and originated from modern day Uzbekistan. He said enough time had passed to turn the Taj Mahal 'Indian.'

Xenophobia and ethnocentrism are familiar ideologies embraced across many parts of Asia. Perhaps the most frightening example of its manifestation is government policies to rationalize genocides via ethnic cleansing from Myanmar to Sri Lanka to India to China. Millions of Uighur people are still in concentration camps in Xinjiang. Racism is an issue of urgency in Asia; in certain cases, it is a matter of life or death.

For all these reasons, discussing racism is always relevant and important. And while positive signs from younger generations show that attitudes about race are evolving, there is still much more work to do. There is so much room to share stories from this continent to challenge discrimination in all forms.

Black in Asia exists as an effort to amplify stories from Black people who have lived in Asia to raise consciousness about the experiences they face while living abroad. The fact that Black people are not represented across Asia in numbers seen in the US or the UK is more the reason why these stories deserve to be cherished and shared. The writers do not attempt to solve racism in Asia, although discrimination of Black people in Asia is common. Instead, they share a glimpse into what it's like to be non-Asian people in Asia to inspire joy, reflection, and self-awareness among all readers. Writers share about their interactions with people in Asia, which range from rejection to confusion, curiosity, and acceptance. Powerful and nuanced, these stories are about many conflicting sentiments—exclusion and generosity, alienation and community, appropriation and appreciation.

I grew up in a very privileged environment in Taipei and didn't know how to talk about race with my peers. I felt as if acknowledging racial differences was taboo in itself. I loved listening to Destiny's Child and TLC, but had no Black friends. It's taken me a long time to unpack some of the racism that I've inherited. I'm not done unpacking it yet and might never finish in this lifetime.

At the time of publishing, the writers and I are still not sure who this book will resonate more with: students in Asia, Black students around the world, or just anyone who wants to learn more about race in Asia. We are eager to find out. Regardless of who picks up this book, thank you for reading.

Many of us feel the need to prove we are not racist when we should wrestle with the fact that we have inevitably inherited racism from our cultures. By trying to constantly disprove our racism, we shove internalized racism under the carpet, unwilling to confront ourselves. I hope this anthology serves as an entryway for people to be vulnerable enough to question the preconceptions they have about Black people, and their subconscious racism towards other groups of people.

One final note about Spill Stories: while Spill Stories is designed consciously for womxn of color, anyone is welcome to share their stories, including women, men, and gender fluid friends. The use of 'womxn' versus 'women' is a gesture of solidarity and inclusivity of trans and non-binary women. If you are interested in writing or collaborating, please contact spillyourstories@gmail.com.

- Tiffany Huang

Table of Contents:

1.
From Saint Lucia to Taipei
By Bernise Springer

I was born and raised in Saint Lucia but began to grow into myself in Taiwan. I've climbed the ranks from a mere student to working professional over the course of six years. The sum of my experiences constitutes a piece of my identity, which is anchored to this place. I will probably tell this story for years to come, as those few days settled and centered my soul in a way that still catches me off guard to this day.

She sold lunch boxes outside my apartment building daily. They were cheap, slightly greasy but all around delicious, so it wasn't a surprise that this was where I got my dinner night after night when I lived on 'Good Fortune and Long Life' Street. She was probably in her late 60s, but she had an ever-youthful energy about her which was probably heightened by my presence as a towering Black woman with a curly fro. I became her friend quickly as evidenced by the fruits she added in my bag or the extra gravy she put on my rice. We would chat from time to time and in typical Taiwanese "a-ma" fashion, I became the show-and-tell to her friends who always seemed to get my name wrong.

"Hey, what are you doing for Chinese New Year?" she asked one day.
The way she asked sounded like it would be best that I didn't have anything planned.
"Oh, nothing really."
"Ok. You come to my house."
That was an order.

Even after mentioning that a friend of mine was coming to visit me from Australia for the New Year, I was simply told that she could come too.

So we did.

My friend and I took lodging at the home of another elderly lady who spoke little Chinese (let alone English) and whose son honestly looked like a gang member. We stayed in his room for the next three days while he slept downstairs.

Chinese New Year rolled around and I was reminded of the warmth of family after being away for what had been two years at the time. From watching 'A-gong' catch fish in the river, to lighting firecrackers at night with the neighbourhood kids, to being cramped around a small round table laden with food made with love -- it was an unforgettable experience especially for my friend and I, who were definitely not the usual sight in this country town. It felt good and freeing. I hope they're well.

2.
From Washington, D.C. to the
outskirts of Seoul
By Erica K. Butler

Living in Korea has given me the opportunity to grow, nurture, and continue to augment myself. It's been a dream of mine to come here and every day when I'm riding my motorcycle, doing taekwondo and speaking Korean, I feel self-assured and invigorated knowing that I am living my dream. With the self-limiting mindset that is present in so many people's psyche, I give myself hope, knowing that if I can do this, I can do anything and everything.

I came to Korea in November of 2018. I was so elated to be here. I love going to different places. Infusing different cultures within myself. When I first came here, it felt like I was in a completely different realm. Truly. And that feeling lasted for months. It wasn't a matter of culture shock; I felt like I had gone to a completely different planet where people were independently thriving.

I thought of my Asian university friends. To this day, I try to make comparisons. I think of Jingwen and how she feels when she sees another American building or park. How Lei must have felt when he moved to high school in Massachusetts and he walked into the cafeteria. I know this cross-cultural experience applies to anyone from any continent going to another. But as I am in Asia and see Asians every day, I only think of this in regard to my Chinese friends. Anyway, enough about them. This is about me. Upon my arrival to Korea, I lived in 김포 (Gimpo city). I proudly consider 김포 사우동 (Sau-dong) my Korean 고향 (hometown). And sans my evil boss, I had a wonderful time there. I go back sometimes with longing in my heart to return. The people that I met there are lovely.

They remember my name - that's important! They talk to me with a genuine smile on their lips. They were there when I broke my foot running, when I bought my bike. They asked me how my healing was. They told the cook that I like my food spicy. They noticed my weight loss. They invited me to their church and their overnight young adult retreat. That was a wonderful week. I felt so loved. Waking up next to these new people. Walking outside to hear the morning birds chirp, see the clothes hanging on the line, all of the trees and grass and crops. I miss my church. I miss 경기도 (Gyeonggi province).

Writing this and looking back at the photos is making me think that I hate living in Seoul. Ah. In 김포 (Gimpo), I felt at home. I didn't get many stares and if I got any, I didn't notice them. People talked to me in Korean. People were kind. And then I crossed the bridge to 일산 (Ilsan) for 태권도 (Taekwando); I made another family. When I moved, I travelled 3 and a half hours to and fro several times a week to remain at my 태권도장 (Taekwondo program). That's how much community means to me once I've found it. Long story short, I think that my most poignant memories are in 경기도 (Gyeonggi).

As for where is home, home is wherever I am. And with 김포 사우동 (Gimpo Saudong) being my 고향 (hometown) of the country I am in, yes, I do miss it. But otherwise, I am happiest here. In Korea.

I have my bike. My freedom. No guns coming to harm my skin. I've lost 50+ pounds here and am still improving. Sometimes I want to be invisible. I have large hips and brown skin, so I know I'm very noticeable because of those two anomalies within Korean society. But other than that, I'm okay. I just hate when people try to talk to me in English.

내 마음은 경기도에서 있다 (My heart is in Gyeonggi).

3.
From Louisiana to Seoul
By Monique Claiborne

I've come to find satisfaction in the convoluted looks of bewilderment, intrigue, and (dare I say) respect on people's faces every time I say I'm from Opelousas, Louisiana. What the hell am I doing in Asia? It simply "doesn't make sense." Well, today marks exactly 3 years since I first made my home in Seoul. I still don't know why I felt compelled to move to Korea, and I'm sure that the tremendous growth I've experienced here could have hypothetically happened elsewhere. All I know is that when I look at the woman I've become since I applied for the fellowship program that would change my life, I am affirmed daily that I am exactly where I am supposed to be.

Being Black in Asia. Being me in the world. It's impossible to separate the two. I'm not sure where my Blackness ends and Mo begins, if my skin informs or determines my identity--whether I'm more like a vibrant city intersection or a signature cocktail whose very essence depends on the delicate balance between mind, matter, and melanin right down to the milliliter.

It is in this unknowing that I have come to learn. My experiences are as true as the narratives I give them, and while I cannot control how others perceive me, their perspectives are only as powerful as my own.

People stare at me in China.
People stare at me in Opelousas.
Men catcall me in India.
Men catcall me in New York.
Dating is hard for Black women in Korea.
Dating is hard for Black women.
I feel quite invisible living in Seoul, which is why I like it, to be honest.
Sometimes I wonder if I should be more disillusioned about the little things that throw some people off.

"Oh, this ahjumma pushed me in the subway!" "Koreans never hold open the door!" Well that ajumma pushed everyone in the subway, and I was the hundredth person that door hit in the face. These little moments make me feel like part of the rhythm, part of the flow that is Seoul, and it's in these everyday "mishaps" that I truly feel like I belong.

I am not one for pleasantries. I don't
need to greet strangers in the elevator,
and I don't miss the small talk of
"southern hospitality." That small talk
comes with a lot of assumptions, usually
shrouded in questions that bring the
biases of Americans to the fore. "Oh, you
went to Princeton. Did you go for
sports?" "Oh, you interned at Google.
Was that for a diversity program?"

No one is asking me pointless shit here.
Koreans be like, "Oh you went to
Princeton. Can you tutor my kid? I'll pay
you a lot of money and bring you
snacks." Um, yes.

On one hand, being Black in Asia has felt
wholly unremarkable, just a
continuation of being a kid in the
American South, a student on the East
Coast, and now an entrepreneur in
South Korea with detours through a
dozen Asian countries along the way.

For me, being Black in Asia has meant
not being Black in America. Since
moving to Korea, the racially charged

questions, comments, anxieties and fears that color every thread of cheap American fabric have retreated into the background. I've chosen to my own fabric and am stitching something different, something uniquely tailored to suit me.

4.
From Congo to Hong Kong
By Harmony "Ann-Marie" Ilunga

I am from the Democratic Republic of Congo and moved to Hong Kong in 2011 as a refugee. Facing discrimination as a model of color, I founded @_harmonyhk_, a modelling agency and social enterprise spotlighting local ethnic minority talents to challenge the lack of diversity in Hong Kong. I am currently an undergraduate student majoring in psychology, a freelance model, and the co-founder of Learning Together, an organization that runs an educational programs for asylum seekers and refugees in Hong Kong.

Being Black and a refugee in a society like Hong Kong has never been easy for me. I get lost on where I belong. I cannot even go back home to my country and I cannot get an identity here in Hong Kong.

No matter how much time I try to make myself feel included as part of Hong Kong society, the people around me don't make me feel that way or acknowledge me, so from time to time, I tell myself I am a global citizen rather than categorising myself as part of a certain group.

It hurts sometimes because I want to have a sense of identity. I am Congolese, but sometimes when I speak to Congolese people back home, they make me feel like a stranger, like I am not 100% Congolese anymore although I feel like it.

When I am in Asia, there is no way I am ever going to feel accepted, but I have learned to accept myself and live in the moment.

That's one of the biggest lessons I have learned. I am a global citizen, and a global citizen belongs wherever they want to belong.

Credits for Harmony's photo are as follows:

Model: @harmony_btd
Makeup: @niharika.sabnani_mua
Designs: @fongbra @jasonlkk @ymdhstudio
Photographer: @bostonmango

5.
From Denver to Seoul
By Melissa Watkins

I'm a writer and educator in South Korea. I've been here a long time and life just feels normal to me now--which is why it's so weird when people say weird things to me based on some alternate stereotypical reality, which I suppose is the inspiration for my piece here. Oh, and if you like to read, please find me on social media @equalopportunityreader. I do reviews, news and discussion about books that center on diverse perspectives and readers across genres. Come find a good book with me! :-)

"Since I've never been anything other than a Black woman, I can't tell you how specifically anything feels any more than someone could tell someone how things feel as a white woman. It's a creepy question. Stop asking it."- Shonda Rhimes

I am normal to myself. Seems simple, right? The idea of being your own default seems an emotional human right. I am myself and always have been, and therefore I define my own default. My definition of normal begins with me and extends outward rather than the other way around. Yet I realize that some people seem to think I see myself as strangely as they see me.

My skin has always been this color. My lips always this shape. My hair, this texture. I am not surprised when I see myself in the mirror. I do not scream at the sight of my own face. I do not need injections and filler. I do not wear my hair only to parties where I take selfies for likes. This is normal. I am normal. You are, too, but don't expect me to push aside my normal to validate yours. Don't invalidate my normal by making it your trend.

Also, don't assume your trend is my normal. I'm Black. I'm a woman. I'm easily defined as both. I am obvious but not consumable. I am not the Black the media told you about. My lip gloss is not popping, my eyebrows are not on fleek, and I cannot twerk without causing minor damage to my lower back and knees. I sound nothing like Beyonce when I sing, cornrows make my scalp itch and if you challenge me to a basketball match, I can only assume you want to win and aren't very good at the game yourself. Whatever rapping ability I may have been genetically entitled to was accidentally given to a white boy with lots of tattoos and half a million TikTok followers. I have no idea how to do that thing you saw in that video and hey, newsflash--being Black is not defined by any of those things.

Black people define being Black—you, and the things you buy to try to be cool, do not.

6.
From Atlanta to Seoul
By Kami Rose

*Living in Asia can be tough when media proceeds
you. Before even forming my mouth to say my
name, some people believe they already know
me. I want to say some preconceived ideas are
positive, such as, "Wow, you must be a good
dancer!" But all preconceived ideas are negative
if they take away my voice and the ability to form
my own identity. I haven't met many who see me
first, but the individuals who give me the
opportunity to be a fresh canvas make a world of
a difference. I mean, I can dance, but give me the
opportunity to show you first.*

black
strange
circus
thing
object
praised
wanted
interesting
monster
thief
ugly
cool
display window

smile
maybe today,
they will just see
you.

7.
From USA to Singapore
By Felicia Iyamu

Here's a short piece shedding light on casual conversations with locals in Singapore from an expat. It should elicit a feeling of nostalgia and perspective, with notes on the subtlety of systems of oppression (feminism, racism, etc.) and how history is taught and learned. Felicia Iyamu is an up and coming contemporary fantasy and historical fiction book series author. Follow her to learn more about the book launch soon, intersectionality, fashion-forward living and an uplifting lifestyle.

Her name was Tina. She came from India—sweet like honey, a mom of two. I had just arrived, and she asked, "What does freedom mean to you?" She laughed a hesitant laugh and I thought I knew.

Following an arranged marriage and expectations, she moved miles away to make it with her man and forge a plan. She learned how to drive and got an unassuming title. She stood on two feet, just in time to meet me. She took me under her broken wing. Immediately, she sang, "Welcome, foreign brown girl, to Singapore. Find your freedom! I'm not sure I did...I'm proud of you." Her name was Tina.

These are friends from different places—faces of different races that could be my face or my brother's face. I couldn't help but think, "Are we all the same?" No. Yes! No...it depends on your point of view. It depends on what door you're peering through.

His name was Esmond. He always hesitated when I walked in. The thought across his face said, "Who is this brown girl with grace?" He talked about Singapore back in the day, but he never mentioned Malay. He talked about Singapore back in the day, but he never acknowledged race. Why?

He asked, "Where in Africa are you from?" I replied, "You're from Africa too. We're all from Africa my dude." He laughed a curious, full belly laugh. Behind his eyes were confusion, aghast. His name was Esmond.

Too many stories to tell. Asia, you've helped me grow, and well, I'm grateful. I'm thankful. I'm courageous, but I've gone through stages. I'm here.

8.
From Louisiana to Bangkok
By Trey Hurst

I'd always wanted to live abroad, so when I was presented with a chance to move to Thailand, I couldn't pass it up. I grew up in the heat and humidity of Louisiana, so steamy Bangkok reminds me of home. Every day I learn something new about Thai culture. Living here has given me an opportunity to better understand myself and examine my own behaviors, beliefs, and biases. I feel like I'm always growing.

I grew up in Baton Rouge, Louisiana and moved to Bangkok three years ago. Before that move, I spent several years living in Chicago, then San Francisco. For me, each place presented a very different version of racism in America (a story for another day).

Even before my move to Thailand, the possibility of encountering racism while abroad was always top of mind. When planning a trip, I would wonder, "What type(s) of racism should I expect?" I would Google "being Black in (insert country)" to get a sense of what I might experience.

I did the same before I moved to Thailand. I read stories from Africans, Black Americans, Black Europeans, and other Black folk who had lived in or visited Thailand. For me, it was important to understand what I might expect as a queer African American. We are not all treated the same. #allBlacklivesmatter

So, what has my experience been like?

Living in Thailand has been good for my soul. For the most part, I've been met with kindness. The good far outweighs the bad, and the experience has helped me reframe what it means to be an American (another tangent I'll avoid).

The way that people think about race here is quite different. The racism I experience is less of a threat to my life.

It often (but not always) stems from fear due to true ignorance and a lack of knowledge or information, rather than flat-out hatred or dehumanization. So, for the past three years, I've felt relatively safe and secure. I can breathe easily.

It doesn't mean that life isn't without its micro aggressions. As I mentioned, the one I experience the most is irrational fear from others.

I can't take the train without at least one person seeing me as a threat and recoiling away from me. I notice it; I can't always ignore the "purse clutch" or someone frantically checking to see if their wallet is still there while staring at me. Over time, this micro-aggression starts to hurt. It's like being poked with a dull needle over and over in the same spot. Eventually, you'll break the skin.

The fear, the insinuation that I am some sort of threat, is hurtful. It makes me so self-conscious about the space I occupy, my body language, and my facial expressions. Getting that look from people has ruined my day a few times.

But again, these are "dull pokes." They are nothing compared to the racism I've experienced growing up in America. So, for now, I'll continue to call Thailand home.

9.
From Detroit to Shanghai
By Tone Twisted

My name is TØNE and I'm an Art Director,
model, and musician from Detroit, Michigan, but
I've spent the past 4 years living in Shanghai.
Since coming to Asia, I have been afforded many
opportunities to show my creativity, from
performing in front of thousands, to writing and
creative directing global commercial projects, to
modeling and walking for some of the biggest
brands during Shanghai Fashion Week. I always
knew that I was destined to be a creative, but I
was unsure how I was going to release that outlet
until one of the most random career switches
happened while living in China - becoming a
model!

Many people may know me as just a
rapper or a fashion influencer. These
very in-demand fields exploded in
popularity over the past few years in
China and I was at the right place at the
right time.

I never ever pictured myself being a
model—like, that was the last thing I
thought I would ever be. I was chubby
and nerdy in high school and more
interested in art and design than fashion
at the time.

So, allow me to list my top 10 wildest experiences being a model/actor in China.

1. I got my very first modeling job walking around aimlessly during my first week of Shanghai and approaching a guy in a Kendrick Lamar t-shirt for directions (he must speak English, right?). This ended up with me on the back of his scooter on my way to the metro station where he introduced himself as a designer and invited me to model for his new brand - and it was all up-hill from there!

2. I was flown down to Shenzhen for a commercial shooting one evening and the client had cancelled the shoot for the morning by around midnight. I was already out partying with some friends and ended up spending the night in a spa/resort. I looked at it like a free vacation. They flew me back a week later to complete the shooting, which never ended up getting released!

3. I was a part of a 4-hour livestream interactive runway show in Beijing that had performances by Jaden Smith and others. It was one of the most viewed events of its kind in history!

4. I was featured on the front page of Taobao (the Chinese Amazon) for a week during a record-breaking sales campaign for popular milk brand WangWang in collaboration with fashion brand TYAKASHA.

5. I rapped on the runway during MISHKA NY at Shanghai Fashion Week S/S 2019.

6. One of the perks of modeling is being able to take home some clothes or some gear after a shoot. Li-Ning gifted me some special 1:1 basketball shoes only made for the runway that I will keep forever in my sneaker collection.

7. Speaking of shoes - I comfortably wear a size 12 (EU 46) and I've had to squeeze into a size 43 before. For taking photos, it

was cool, but walking was literally torture!

8. I've literally gotten jobs just because of the color of my skin - I have had numerous basketball roles and my friends will tell you, I can't hoop for my life! Also, I've gotten jobs because they mistakenly assume I'm the "other guy with dreads."

9. One time, an agent asked me if I was grateful for slavery because if it weren't for the genetic mixing, I "wouldn't be so beautiful." I had no idea how to respond to that, but I took it as a backhanded compliment. These "micro-aggressions" occur on a daily basis in China. Casting calls ask for "chocolate skin models" or "not too Black but dark skinned required," or they even ask for "wheat skin" —like, what color is that even? I don't personally take this offensively or even as racist, but I hope that over time, some awareness and cultural sensitivity is developed as the foreign talent industry expands in Asia.

10. I almost led a mutiny of male models in Guangzhou when the booker tried to play us on the money. Long story short, I let the other models know and exercise their rights so that they could demand their rightful wage and not be bullied or coerced into accepting less. I have a Bachelors in Industrial & Labor Relations with a focus in Human Resources from Cornell University, which I surprisingly end up using on a daily basis when it comes to negotiating deals and representing myself as an independent contractor. I have a passion for workers' rights and representation, which naturally segues into my current ventures of A&R, Talent Management and Artist Development.

Overall, I have had quite a wild ride and my experience as a model influenced my current trajectory immensely. Shanghai has certainly been the launching pad to my career and a playground to learn, explore, and find my unique place in this industry.

10.
The Earth Is Not Ours
By: Lois Orekoya

Born in Nigeria, I grew up in Singapore,
Chengdu, China, Suriname, and now, Hong Kong.
I answer "Where are you from?" questions
usually like that. I've lived mostly in Asian
culture and countries for my entire life. This
piece is inspired by the journey of being different
everywhere you go. And how that's what makes
you, you.

I've never been the same as others. I've always been a little different than the humans around me, whether in language, mindset, skin-tone or my own mixed culture. There's something unique about living in four different and distinct locations my whole life, three Asian, all foreign to my bloodline. I was born in Nigeria, a country filled with potential, but I can't fully connect to it. Having left at age 1, I still can't claim to fully connect to any of the other places: Singapore, Chengdu, China, Suriname, and now, Hong Kong.

I've grown through the stares and the fears, the tears, and the years of isolation and never really fitting in. I've grown through the Sichuan food, chicken rice,

pasta, jollof rice, satay, noodle soups -
and fried mantou. I've grown through
the joyful days and hangouts with people
from all over the world. I've grown
through birthday parties I'd never forget.
I grew through a childhood that I was
blessed to live. But I still feel the
microaggressions and pains of growing
while in constant transition today.

I've never been the same, and I've grown
to accept it—that's okay. This creates
new cultures and perspectives, like a
hidden garden coming to light. And I've
learned that being different is being you.

I hope each of us have the opportunity to
live our own lives, unique, loved and
seen. No matter how different we may
be. I constantly tell myself 'I belong here'
even when everything tells me I don't. I
somehow still believe I belong anywhere
because I know what it's like to be
home—it's when I'm in nature. It's
something that no human owns. Nature,
no matter in which country, doesn't
belong to humanity. It's a part of our
world.

It's a world that also doesn't belong to a culture, or a background or an ethnicity, yet holds all of us, whether the same or different. So maybe I'll never be the same. Maybe I'll speak Mandarin and Cantonese, maybe I'll remember some Dutch and Korean from the K-Dramas I watch with my mom, maybe I'll find gong bao ji ding and lasagne as comfort foods, and maybe I'll have a diverse culture and never feel one place could really be my home....maybe I'll keep on feeling like I'm not the same, and that's okay.

None of us are exactly the same.

11.
When Buddha and Jesus Met
By Bernise Springer

Fun fact: I experienced colorism before I even knew the word for it. As a child growing up in the Caribbean island of Saint Lucia, this was one of my silent struggles—a poignant reminder that even in a country where the majority of people looked like me, the undertones of its colonial past still carried through seemingly harmless experiences regarding skin tone. That being said, I've never been as comfortable in this melanin skin as I am now. It's the type of comfort where I make sure that the lotion I buy has no whitening agent, where I only stand in the shade to avoid a heatstroke from Taiwan's summer sun, and where the clothes and colors I wear celebrate the skin that adorns me.

I'm Christian, but I often imagined Buddha and Jesus having conversations from time to time about us wee folk down here on earth. I would frequently picture the two of them casually commenting on the day to day happenings of the life of a random soul:

"Do you remember this guy? He almost missed the bus for that interview at Ernst & Young 2 months ago. His mom put in a request to me for him."

"Ah yes, I remember him --I saw the whole thing. I'm happy for him, but I hope that he can at least stop to see his sick aunt in hospice before she passes, you know? Time waits for no man."
"Word."

Something like that.

I'm sure that there were moments when they bickered, times that they found common ground, and when agreeing to disagree was the best way to keep the peace. Think about the commentary that ensued when they each recounted how they crossed paths with the other's followers. Stories for ages to come, I reckon.

And mine is no different.

I met Buddha through an "upper-aged woman" who sold souvenirs at this little shop in Taiwan's mystical mountain village of Jiufen. She, after finding out that I was hoping to find a job in Taiwan, offered to pray for me. She took me to where he stood at the entrance of the shop carved in wood, polished and adorned. Her prayer, spoken in Mandarin Chinese, was punctuated by subtle bows and went something like this:

"Please make her skin lighter and her hair longer so that she can find a job in Taiwan. Amituofo (阿彌陀佛)."

I believed that she had the best intention, but that execution though...

Bruh.

As I lie here several years later, waiting for sleep to creep to prepare me for an early start to my workday, I'm grateful for this unanswered prayer. Save the length of my hair, my melanin is still as deep and as rich as it was back then. Who knows, maybe that unanswered prayer was one of those times where Jesus and Buddha both looked down and said...

"Nah, she good."

12.
Growing up in Japan
By Charnell McQueen

I am Charnell, a designer based out of the Bay Area. I grew up across many countries, including Japan. Recently, I went to visit my mom and take a break from the city. It took about five weeks to break out the photos upon photos that my mom had taken over her life. And it had been a long time since I had seen them. The photo negatives and the yellow envelopes that hold memories and moments. My favorite photos were the ones of me growing up in Japan. I held those photos the longest as my mom recounted places we had gone and the adventures we had.

Recently, I went to visit my mom and take a break from the city.

It took about five weeks to break out the photos upon photos that my mom had taken over her life. And it had been a long time since I had seen them. The photo negatives and the yellow envelopes that hold memories and moments. My favorite photos were the ones of me growing up in Japan. I held those photos the longest as my mom recounted places we had gone and the adventures we had.

My earliest memories of my childhood have always been set in Japan.

My dad was a Staff Sergeant in the Air Force and had been stationed at Yokota Air Force Base, Japan. We moved there when I was around one year old and stayed for five and a half years. For a little over a year, we lived off the military base before housing became available. I remember our small apartment, filled with many sliding screen doors and hardwood floors. My dad worked at the legal office and my mom taught English at a neighboring primary school.

It's weird looking back on your childhood, especially in pictures. You can pinpoint different parts of the day, remember the people, or even a specific toy, and laugh at the outfits that were in style at the time. *So much paisley print!*

Lately, I've been navigating these feelings and memories of nostalgia. Every day, I would set off with my mom to go to her work. I would sit behind her desk, sometimes paying attention to the lessons she taught the other students or other times reading and working on my activity books. My mornings were filled with thousands of hours of English lessons which in reality weren't that much, but to a child, they were not fun at all. But recess—recess was my favorite time of the day. No work, just play.

Being the only Black kid, of course, I knew I was different from everyone else at my Japanese international school. I was reminded of this every time we left our home. People would stop my family to take pictures of us. *I admit my family's drip was amazing but the surprise photo ops happened because the Japanese strangers, literal people who were on the street, had never seen Black people before.* Anytime my dad would dance in public people would say he was Michael Jackson because he could moonwalk. *Not all Black people look alike; insert eye-roll.* And don't even get me started on the numerous times people would. Touch. My. Hair. *In my thesis, I will explain why you should never touch a Black woman's hair.*

I made friendships on the jungle-gym. Despite the interactions I had in the world outside of the classroom, my mother's students became my friends. We would pass notes when my mom was handing out assignments and share candy they had gotten from other teachers and soon I was asking my mom if I could go play with my new friends after school. I was welcomed into their homes during holidays and family events. I remember learning about my friends' different traditions, trying new foods, and learning new words and phrases for everything around me.

One day after leaving the playground, my mom caught me speaking Japanese to one of my friends. She likes to remind me of this moment any time we're talking about Japan: "I heard you talking to your friends on the playground in Japanese. And I asked you, 'Charnell, are you speaking Japanese? When did you learn to speak Japanese!'" and my reply was very matter-of-fact for a four-year-old, stating, "I learned it from my friends, Mommy. I teach them English and they teach me Japanese."

I think what surprised my mom the most was that despite the negative interactions we had outside our home and her classroom, I learned another language. Childhood me wanted to learn more about Japanese culture even though I was looked at like a foreign body.

Of course, now all I can do is count and pick up on some things here and there, but I used to be fluent, I swear!

Years later, I still remember when the cherry blossom petals that smelled so sweet colored the streets light pink. I remember the intense beat of the taiko drums being played during summer festivals and colorful dragons dancing in the parades. I remember my friend's grandmother teaching us how to conduct a Japanese tea ceremony at the age of five. I remember my friends Sasha and Christine, who went by their American names on base at school but by their Japanese names at home.

Japan will always be my first home, filled with positive and negative memories of culture and community that will always be a part of me. Those experiences influenced who I am today. It's weird looking back on your childhood, especially in pictures. I mentioned growing up in Japan to one of my friends, Emeric, and we talked about nostalgia and childhood innocence — how things we loved and held dear to us are uncovered with words we didn't know before that describe the problematic structures of society.

Emeric said, "Those experiences in your childhood are real, and the older you get the more the meanings of those experiences expand." And that really stuck with me.

The fantastical memories were shown in a new light.

Yes, there were smiling moments captured on camera but there were also moments of eye-rolls, anger and frustration that need to be remembered too. This fact doesn't ruin the memory but develops it. It brings growth and dimensionality to the present, and it brings realism and accountability to the communities I call home.

13.
From New Jersey to Myanmar
By Jessica O. Acholonu

I'm a writer, teacher, and travel enthusiast. Ask almost any Black person, man or woman, about their hair care routine or do a search for Black hair tutorials online, and you'll begin to get a sense of how important hair is to our community. When I decided to move abroad long term, I had to get a little innovative in order to maintain it. This is an ode to those experiences, and learning and understanding along the way.

I am a first generation American, born of two Nigerian parents from Igboland. So, I think, I have always lived a life of duality, of double consciousness, like the sort that W.E.B DuBois talks about.

I had grown up, lived, and worked within the same 20-mile radius my entire life. After teaching for 4 years in New Jersey, it was time to shake things up. I'm not sure what I was expecting, or if I was expecting anything at all when I moved to Myanmar. I remember thinking of how it reminded me of Nigeria in some ways when I first landed. For a time, I took comfort in that familiarity. But the nostalgia wears away.

I think I can mark almost exactly when that happened. It was when I ran out of the hair products I lugged 7,000 miles from the US to Myanmar. What I hadn't planned for when I moved to Myanmar was how the environment would impact my typical wash, condition, deep condition, leave-in conditioner, cream, oil-to-seal-in-the-moisturizer routine.

The water quality is harsh, leaving my high porosity 4b/4c hair too dry and brittle. The constant heat added to the dryness, plus the high AQI meant washing my hair far more frequently. Before I knew it, my products were gone.

A lot of my identity is wrapped up in my hair, which is no surprise, when Black hair is so often politicized and criticized. It wasn't until I moved to Myanmar that I was confronted with the idea that maybe I didn't know how to really—and I mean, really—take care of my hair after all. Even in the US, it's only been within the last decade or so that Black hair has become mainstream enough that big corporations could bother themselves with stocking their shelves with products that cater specifically to us.

With no products available, I became a kitchen chemist, scouring the internet for DIY deep conditioners, leave-in conditioners, and moisturizers that I could make on my own with items I could find here—some with greater success than others.

The coconut milk, water, and rosemary oil mix leave-in conditioner left my hair feeling soft and luxurious, but its short shelf life wasn't ideal for a busy life or travel. The banana, avocado, and yogurt deep conditioner recipe was awful and left banana pulp in my kinky/ coily hair for at least a week, even after multiple washes.

Eventually, the universe intervened. A friend was off to New York. I begged him to bring me back some shea butter, which is a fat extracted from the nut of the African shea tree, native to West

Africa and a cornerstone of Black hair care.

Having raw shea butter became a pivotal moment. My antics as a kitchen chemist continued, but so did my research. When my sister came to visit, I had her bring chebe powder, which originates from the Republic of Chad, a border nation to Nigeria. These two products together, along with a few others, have kept my hair moisturized for far longer than anything I have ever purchased in the store.

For as long as I decide to live abroad, hair care will always be a top consideration for where I go and/or how I pack. In some ways, these two years in Myanmar have taken me back to a part of my roots, forced me to think more sustainably, and to live a little more simply.

14.
From Nigeria to Mongolia
By Oni Aningo

I am writing about my adventures in Mongolia as a journalist. I am the founder and creator of the Rising Woman Series on NBC. I am also the author of My Real Name Is, *a photo prose coffee table book on identity, culture and reclaiming it. I am currently working on a series of coloring books, starting with one of Mongolia's queens.*

Being an African womanist in Asia, I have a survival strategy comprised of three phrases: thank you, good morning, and excuse me please.

I use the word African instead of Black because I truly do feel African—an African where we are white with blue eyes, an African where we are brown with green eyes and brown hair, an African where we are so Black we are blue (blue Black) with blonde hair, an African that resonates with our hearts and not with our various colors. This mindset is what has carried me till today against all odds, while being constantly reminded that I am a Black woman, and the biases of it all. I am not naïve.

I am not a risk taker, but there is something about travel that makes me want to go to the most extreme places in the world without feeling lost. When I worked in the Middle East, my first assignment was in Qatar, then an unknown gulf peninsula that everyone thought was Saudi Arabia or Kuwait. And since then, I realized that I only needed to know a few words in every language to get by.

My first time in Asia was when I chose a mining report assignment to live and work in Mongolia for five months in 2012. I figured that if I was going to be in the mining sector, I better take this assignment in Mongolia, a country with the largest gold, copper and coal porphyries in the world. It was an opportunity of a lifetime. I wanted to be in the mines, and I wanted to understand the difference between greenfield and brownfield investments.

I had never been to Asia before and yet, I chose Mongolia, instead of working in Hong Kong, Japan, or China. It was the same way I worked and lived in Qatar instead of in Dubai or Saudi Arabia in 2007.

In 2012, I had been working internationally for 5 years and perfected my formula for travel worldwide. I am African but possess an American passport, for which I am grateful because it made travel easier. All I ever needed was what I call System A: my passport, a visa, my credit card, and a few hundred-dollar bills. I almost always travelled alone and hopped into a taxi or a chauffeured car to my hotel or apartment.

Asia was a shock to me, especially extreme Mongolia. It took me 2-3 days to get to Ulaanbaatar. I rarely researched on culture, people, being Black, or being female in my assigned countries. Instead, I focused on the country's current economic, political and investment status; after all, that was my mission. I also devised system B upon arrival, which helped me stay in the country. With a disarming smile and direct eye contact, I only had to know 3 phrases in every language to thrive.

In Mongolia, it was always bayarlalaa (thank you) for me. Everywhere I went, I held my head high, because I knew I stood out and could not afford to cower in obscurity. A Black woman at 5 feet 8 inches, I stood at 6 feet tall in heels. In Asia, I learned how to embrace my differences. Bayarlalaa was my go-to word for everything. I focused on Ulaanbaatar's qualities rather than its challenges: the wide expanse of blue sky, which I have only otherwise seen in Cape Town, the stark terrain, the sharp cold air—even in its July summers, the air was crisp. The people were beautiful, honest, proud, and stoic. Oh, and they loved their vodka. They even had Genghis Khan vodka.

I had to travel to Hong Kong a few times, after which I spent a few months living there. To me, Hong Kong felt like New York on steroids. No one had time for good mornings, and so I quickly adopted chengmahn (excuse me please) for directions, before I asked a question, for recommendations, and so forth. In Korea, courtesy is paramount, and so I found myself combining my 3-phrase formula system: annyeonghaseyo (good morning), sillyehabnida (excuse me please), and kamsahamnida (thank you). System A and B always work.

I also learned discipline, how to be silent, and that you can practice Tai chi in the middle of a boisterous city. I came to love kimchi and seaweed, and I found that Mongolian beef is actually a myth fabricated by the Chinese. There is no Mongolian beef in Mongolia.

Because of Covid, I am in my home in Lagos, Nigeria, where I find myself ordering kimchi with rice and delicious salted side dishes while drinking soju and somaek. Korean food is my favorite food. My Netflix history is loaded with K- dramas. I just can't seem to get enough of Jung Il-woo and Lee Min-ho, my two favorite actors. I have been to more than 50 countries and yet, I find myself nostalgic about places where I've lived in Asia. I plan to go back to Korea for its design, fashion, and skincare, and Mongolia to feel the expanse of the Gobi Desert, crisp and stark. And those blue skies you cannot find anywhere else in the world. Every time I land in an airport, I look up at the skies, and think of the Mongolian blue skies, searching for a comparison. There is none.

In the Gobi deserts, I learned to be quiet, to be still, and to be resilient. I carry that till today, especially now, when we have all experienced isolation. Now, more than ever, I close my eyes, and I am in a yurt, drinking airag in the expanse of lands upon lands, reveling in the beauty of stillness and quiet. I need this now to qualm the fears I sometimes find myself in, with isolation and social distancing. Bayarlalaa Mongolia, Bayarlalaa Asia.

15.
From New Jersey to Seoul
By Renée Simone

If it's really hard to argue which came first, the chicken or the egg, let's acknowledge that both have their validity. I am no more or less Liberian than American, Black woman than woman, artist than human. These narratives help me tell my story but never stand alone. I have had the privilege of traveling and living outside of my comfort zone and home country, no these are not synonymous. I am Renée Simone, the Artist. I am Renée Simone, the Creator.

I start my story with my parents, born and raised in Liberia. They came to America for a better life, like most immigrant stories go. They gave birth to me, a daughter who would never lack what they had growing up, or so they thought.

What life never tells you is how the future will unfold. My parents left Liberia in search for a fair country filled with limitless opportunities. For some, America is that country, but for people of color, especially immigrants of color, it is a land filled with hopes and dreams on the false pre-tense that all are created equal and can achieve them justly. Living amidst systemic racism and inequality made me want to search for an alternative to the American dream.

And so here I was, the Liberian-American female born with a French/Latin first name (Renée: "Born Again"), growing up bicultural (Liberian and American), with religious social constructs reinforced by my middle name (Simone "God had heard"), learning how to handle the fact that these poorly crafted boxes would never define me.

So, I took a risk, which has always been my way of life. If I wanted to see the world outside of America as the first-generation token Black girl who graduated with honors to make her family proud, I had to believe in myself and believe I deserved to find my happiness.

So, I did the very thing I had been dreaming of since my childhood. I packed up and moved abroad. Over the last four years, I have lived across Beijing, Shanghai, and Seoul, and have traveled to many other cities. However, there are some reassuring familiarities they share in common: otherness, vulnerability, and growth.

In a place where I am not the majority nor the known, I can speak for myself, be myself, and correct those who prejudge me. In the process of standing up for myself, I became more vocal about how I wanted my life to be: Renée Simone, the Artist. Renée Simone, the Creator.

I was born a Black child, raised a Black child, and will hopefully encourage other Black children to not just be the stereotypes people, media, society tell them they are. It's okay to shape shift to fit those boxes. But if you ever find yourself uncomfortable, well then darling, stretch your limbs and break free.

Yes, I am Black. Yes, I am African. Yes, I am American. Yes, I am human. If you are confused as to how to categorize me, that is a personal problem. I do hope you solve it. No, you cannot touch my hair without asking (a few nice ahjummas will ask out of curiosity). No, you cannot assume I know everything there is to know about America and hip-hop. No. Although I am Black, I do not fit the diversity quota for your brand. Please hire more diverse models. No, I will not twerk for you just because you bought me a drink.

Seoul, you have taught me lots of lessons and I have grown not only as a human but as an artist here. I know that as time goes on, it will only get better. It seems I was well named: the universe heard my prayers for rebirth. And so it was.

Credits for Renée's photo are as follows:

Model: @reneedreamsart
Hair: @eunjianna_
Styling & makeup: @honghanseok
Flower art, prop: @hanseokhong @judybootykim
Photographer: @studiotamdil
Photo assistant & video: @dancingdean

16.
From Seattle to Myanmar
By Bryce Harvey

I've always had a thirst for adventure for as long as I can remember. Growing up in Seattle, Washington, I moved to upstate New York for culinary school, then Rhode Island for my MBA, and then New York City for the start of my career. Along my travels, I was exposed to varying pre-conceived notions about self-identity during a time when I was still figuring it all out.

In 2018 while working in NYC, I decided to follow my wandering spirit once again and take a chance at love, moving to Myanmar to be with my current boyfriend of three years. Living in Myanmar for the past two years gave me the wonderful opportunity to conceptualize and execute a farm-to-table restaurant specializing in seasonally grown local ingredients. Personally, my journey in Myanmar has taught me more than the immersive experience of another country and culture; it has brought me on the path of self-acceptance. Here is a short look into what I've experienced so far on that journey to meet "me."

Coming to Myanmar, I didn't experience strong culture shock like most expats do, because I knew a bit about the country before moving here. I embraced the culture and way of life in Yangon, but I struggled to make social connections. Back home, I came from a strong community and had anticipated some form of that here. In my isolation, I had more of a "social shock," one could say.

Being a Black American and living in Myanmar has been less about my culture and more about "where am I from." Getting asked that question repeatedly has given me some perspective to think about, as I am used to only asking myself, "Where am I going?"

Burmese people have embraced me with the warmest hospitality. They are proud, friendly, and giving. I've enjoyed drinking Toddy liquor made from local palm trees, and sharing snacks and sweet teas with newly made friends.

Whether I am walking downtown near Bogyoke Market, or wandering through People's Park near Shwedagon Pagoda, I am met with smiles and friendly waves. I stay humbled and open when faced with usual questions such as, "Are you

African?" or "You look Middle Eastern, are you?" or "Are you Hispanic?" People have asked me if I am a professional football player. I laugh and respond, "If I had proper coordination, I could be." On one particular rainy night, a taxi driver spoke to me and said, "You have thick curly hair and dark skin. You must be a Negro right?"

I don't take offense to these questions because they are not coming from a place of hurt. With my dark features, curly hair and brown skin, I know I stand out and I love it. These characteristics shape all that I am.

Through it all, I take these questions as acts of genuine interest into my identity during these brief interactions. Navigating a foreign country can be tough. Oftentimes taking a moment to fully open yourself up to the surroundings will come to shape you. For each step forward, I learn the unfamiliar and stand up to rising challenges, all the while embracing the facets that define me.

17.
From Zimbabwe to Hong Kong
By Kemikal Kris

I was born in Zimbabwe and raised by Nigerian parents around several countries, including Russia, before moving to Hong Kong. I'm a teacher during the day, and an artist at night. I'm also one of the co-founders of the events company known as @mamatoldme852, a platform for hip hop artists based in Hong Kong to showcase their talents.

I was born in Zimbabwe to Nigerian parents. Prior to moving to Hong Kong, I lived in several countries due to my dad's job as a diplomat of Nigeria. The last 11 years of my life were spent between Russia and Hong Kong.

People have a lot of stereotypes about Russia, but they weren't reflected in my personal experiences. I enrolled in a language school for about a year before joining a university to study chemical engineering.

It's impossible to live in Russia without being able to speak the language. My experiences before and after becoming fluent in Russian were very different. Before, life was lonely. After, I found that Russians are naturally very friendly people, which surprised me due to the stereotypes from before. Russians are curious people who love to learn about other cultures.

There is racism in Russia just like there is in other European countries. I had foreign friends who dreaded living there, and I had foreign friends who loved living there. The difference between the two was mainly their ability to speak the language. I never had any racist encounters in school. Most of my classmates were very loving. Teachers were very patient towards foreign students.

Fast forward to Hong Kong, where I've been for the last six years. In both countries, I always feel like a visitor because people stare at me all the time. This is understandable because there aren't that many people of colour in both of these countries.

Racism exists everywhere but in different forms. When a Russian is racist, it tends to be towards all foreigners, and they tell you straight to your face that they don't want you here. The racist encounters that I experienced were mostly by illiterate citizens on the streets shouting out racial slurs.

In Hong Kong, racism tends to be towards people of colour--Black and brown, to be exact. For some reason, I tend to feel it more here due to the non-confrontational nature of Hong Kong people.

I don't have the answers to solving racism. I do, however, strongly believe that in order to reduce this problem, educators in primary and secondary institutions have a major role to play. World history should be compulsory in school syllabuses all over the world, and teachers must make it a top priority to enlighten students at a young age that discrimination in any form is unacceptable.

As of now, I currently work as a filmmaking and drama teacher in a local school during the day. I organise events on the side providing a platform for hip hop artists like myself to showcase our talents during the weekends, usually every 1-2 months.

I try to maximise my position as a teacher and event organiser to enlighten my students and guests at my events. With students, I try not to come on too strongly, because most of my students are pretty young (primary - secondary school level). There's usually a lack of interest in these discussions, but I always gravitate to the few who do show interest in learning about other cultures.

Through simple one-on-one communication, I might tell them why it isn't ok to label groups of people with certain words, or why benefiting from a culture that is non-Chinese without studying the history of where or who it stems from is a form of ignorance. Through music, it could be through a song lyric. I won't make an entire song about race for example, because people tend to get turned off by that. To discuss these issues with this generation, we need to be subtle and patient. There's no point getting upset due to people's lack of awareness. Sometimes, I do, but I take a deep breath in those situations and think of the overall picture, and what am I trying to achieve by having these discussions.

18.
Black Hair is Black Pride
By Whitney Cele

My name is Whitney Cele, and I am from South Africa. I have been living and teaching English in Taiwan for 17 months. I left my home because I needed to rediscover who I really was, and my time in Asia has reawakened me to the realities (both painful and glorious) of living whilst Black. Through my blog, "Let Me Tell You a Story", I am exploring vulnerability by sharing my experiences through a retrospective and microscopic lens (check out the link in @whit_cele's bio)!

"Going natural" was never my intention. For most of my adolescence, I had sported short, relaxed hair which I loved for its simplicity and ease. However, constantly dyeing my hair eventually wore it out! You see, at this specific point in my life, Rihanna was my spirit animal and I would dutifully change my hair color to fit her album covers.

Consequently, I wasn't left with much choice but to shave it all off and return to University with a Black Girl Buzzcut—cringe! Long story short, I never chemically straightened my hair again and grew to love my kink despite its difficulty and the societal resistance I experienced because of it. I enjoyed the fact that my natural hair could make people feel some type of way and over time, it became central to my identity and "personal brand."

When I relocated to Taiwan, I did not fully process what moving through this new society with natural, black hair would feel like. I arrived here with long, black, medium-sized Senegalese twists which were the talk of my school. How beautiful I was! The attention was both flattering and exhausting but little did I know just how short-lived the adoration would be.

Seven weeks later, I removed my twists and proudly rocked my natural 4C fro to work. From the moment I set foot in the building, the amused and confused stares and giggles slowly and effectively chipped away at my confidence. Throughout my day, students of all ages pointed at my hair and openly commented on how funny and ugly it was. Although I knew no Chinese, it was not difficult to decode the classroom banter about how ugly the teacher actually was.

This wasn't the first time in my life that I had been openly and publicly ridiculed for having an afro, but it was the first time in which the ridicule was so closely attached to my identity as a Black person and thus felt like an attack on my personhood and value. All of a sudden, students who were intrigued by my presence in class, disassociated, and I lost both respect and authority. Classes that were difficult to handle were now unruly, and great classes stopped listening to and engaging me. Teachers stole glances at me throughout the week and regularly attempted to touch my hair to confirm its authenticity. I went home in tears most days of that week despite the many affirmations I gave myself.

And so it goes, almost two years in, my riding of this pendulum between celebration and abhorrence. Habitually, I have to re-assert my place as both human and teacher whenever I choose to show up as myself in my truest and purest form. My hair is now not only controversial, but it is now also an act of defiance. I refuse to shrink because of how my kids perceive my hair to be, and I refuse to appease them by constantly braiding it. I can only hope one day, they can accept it and thus accept me, but if they don't, that's okay too.

19.
From New York to Seoul
By Dyondra Wilson

I'm a wanderlust writer who teaches English in South Korea. I struggled to move my three and a half suitcases from New York to the small quaint city of Gimcheon where I live now, but I wouldn't have it any other way. Adjusting through life and its many growing pains, I chose to navigate my mid 20's in a foreign land. My scope of the world has never been one dimensional, and after feeling the weight of the world as a Black woman in America, I wanted to shift that weight and feel it somewhere else.

I always wanted to travel the world. As cliché, as it sounds, no one could tell me otherwise.

I wish I could say I came to South Korea on a whim or by chance, or some magical thing shifted in the world and I said, "Yes, Korea is the one." Those statements would be lies, because I manifested my life abroad with the help of God, but I never knew Korea would be the destination. I've always been intrigued by Asian culture, but I was never a K-pop fan. I never obsessed over certain dramas or anime like my friends did. Ever since I could remember, I wanted to travel the world, so I feel that in my heart, God answered one of my deepest desires.

After college, I knew I didn't want to stay at home, and jumping states wasn't enough for me. I wanted to evolve, because prematurely, a part of me already did after losing my little brother.

After his passing, time moved on, but I was still searching for something more. When I finally got my passport, I cried. Traveling and seeing the world was all a dream until it was real.

I finally got on a plane and flew to the other side of the world back in 2016 to study journalism abroad at Dongguk University, while still being connected to my home school program. I made some of my closest college friends during my program. Seoul was kind of a random choice because that's what my university's School of Journalism was offering for that summer, so I just jumped at the opportunity.

Fast forward to 2019, and I'm back three years later in the same country working as a high school English teacher.

South Korea has forced me to find the serendipity in the little things and has become now, more than ever, a second home. I say this because last week I was in the hospital dealing with a horrible stomach infection for six days. Since the single rooms were fully occupied, I had to share a hospital room with four other women. Yes, six days of my life were spent with middle-aged Korean women watching me eat and me watching them eat, snore, laugh, and pass gas all in the same room. These were four women who I didn't know in my small city of Gimcheon, but felt somewhat bonded to after my experience there.

For my first two days in the hospital, I couldn't eat or even drink water. By the third afternoon, the doctor came in and said I could finally eat. When they brought a pink tray of food to my bed, my face lit up and curved upwards into a smile as the four women cheered for me.

As I took the lids off of each dish, I had never been so happy to see rice porridge in my life, until rice porridge became my life for the next three days. Not knowing I needed to bring my own utensils, I was lucky when one of the four women offered me one of her extras. That day broke the ice between us, as I tried to communicate with them the best I could with my broken Korean and body language. I tried to guess what each woman was personally dealing with (besides a patient like me), but all I could tell was that two of the four women may have had similar symptoms due to our matching pink food trays, while the others had white. One of the women pointed to me as she rubbed her stomach, signalling that she, too, had similar stomach issues. Some days, we would laugh at random nuances, and on other days, I would be annoyed when they would keep the TV on too long at night. Through it all, we shared one common room and one common denominator kept us there, which forced us to adapt to each other.

On my last day, I typed a note in one of my apps so that it could translate my farewell message from English to Korean: "Get better and I wish you well." I went to each of the women so they could read it. One made a heart with her fingers, while another nodded her head with her eyes slightly wet.

Ultimately, living in Korea has been the next challenge that's shown me that I can adapt to anything as a Black woman. After my brother passed, I vowed to travel and do all that he couldn't. Knowing what he went through, I was never naive that our mortality was ever truly our 'own'. We can come and go at any moment but living abroad in Asia has allowed me to live. From the good to the bad, I wouldn't trade my life for what it's bloomed into now. I anticipate the unwritten chapters to come.

20.
From Librarian to ESL Teacher
By Erica Tyler

*I'm an ESL Teacher currently living in Thủ Dầu
Một, Vietnam. I have encountered some subtle
and not so subtle racism. Regardless, you can't
let other people's insecurities stop you from
seeing the world.*

I blame National Geographic. When I
was little, my aunts would give me their
old National Geographic magazines. I
was enthralled by the amazing stories of
far off places. I wanted to be an
adventurer. I was always exploring the
hills and abandoned tunnels around our
house in Moorpark, California. I became
interested in Japanese culture during
high school. I wanted to try something
completely different. My teacher really
fostered my love for the language.

Things fell apart when I got married at
19. It was an abusive relationship and I
felt like I had no way out. Education had
always been a huge part of my family
dynamic growing up. But any talk of me
wanting to start a degree ended in
threats and crying that I was just trying
to leave him. I finally managed to return

to school at the age of 29. I felt so out of place. What was I doing here with all these young kids? I was going through a nasty divorce during my first semester and almost flunked out. But I remember the exact day and even the weather when I swore to my friends that I was not going to let feeling sorry for myself stop me from succeeding. I deserved better.

I enrolled in Japanese classes and aced them. The director of the department took notice and kept pushing me to take part in speaking contests. I won both at my university and placed 3rd at Duke. I got accepted into a scholarship program to study abroad in Ōita, Japan. When I told the director of the anthropology department (my second major), the first thing out of her mouth wasn't "Congrats," but rather, "You know they're racist in Japan, right?" In my head, I was thinking, "And it would be different from here how?" So glad I ignored her. Japan was amazing! Upon my return, I spoke regularly at high schools to encourage kids of color to study abroad. I also helped them with finding scholarships.

I decided to go to graduate school instead of going back overseas. My first love will always be books. I was a librarian for a few years. All the while I still dreamt about international travel. I started to follow a lot of amazing travelers on Instagram who were people of color. Seeing their adventures relit that fire within me. I started to research options. Teaching English kept coming up. I was dubious. I wasn't sure if I even liked children (don't worry. I LOVE my students!). I had already lived in Japan and wanted to try a new country. I was too old for South Korea (their loss), and there seemed to be an oversaturation of ESL teachers in Thailand. I was looking at a comparative country chart and thought "Hm, Vietnam looks pretty cool. Beautiful country. Stable economy. Low cost of living. High demand for ESL teachers. Let's do it."

I have been living in Vietnam for about three years. I never thought I would be a teacher. I love living here. Of course, it has its pros and cons as with any part of the world. I have had to deal with subtle and not-so-subtle racism, mostly from other teachers in the industry. When I first moved here, there was only one other Black woman at my company. Thankfully the good outweighs the bad. One of my favorite stories is that one night, my crappy motorbike broke down and I was still 20 minutes from home. I started pushing my bike and of course, it started to rain. As I was pushing and cussing, a motorbike kept passing me. I thought "Oh no, what now?" It was a man and his daughter. She spoke a little English and said her dad was worried about me pushing my bike home so late and wanted to help. He called his friend who picked up my bike. I rode to their home and drank tea with the grandma, chatting poorly in Vietnamese through Google Translate, while they fixed my bike. Afterward, they refused to take any money.

I have been able to travel to the places that I saw in those National Geographic magazines years ago. And I have met some amazing human beings. Every day I wake up here, I am grateful that I didn't give up and let other people's opinions stop me from seeing the world.

21.
From New York City
to Chengdu
to Singapore
By Triston Francis

I am 10,000 miles away from where I was born, living a life I never could have imagined as a child. Having never stepped foot in Singapore prior to landing with my suitcases, I was eager to see what this leap of faith had in store. Being abroad has afforded me a tremendous opportunity to introspect and I could not be happier with the decision.

Throughout childhood, I was forced to grapple with race and identity. My father is a black man from Jamaica and my mother a white woman from Cleveland with Russian and Czech roots.

Regardless of which parent picked me up from school, my classmates would stare. In their minds, I was too dark and my hair too curly for me to be my mom's son, and they felt my skin was not nearly dark enough to match my father.

At age of 11, I started boarding school in Deerfield, Massachusetts. My older brother and I made up roughly 30% of the black population on campus. Once again, race & identity made its way to the top of my mind.

From this point forward, I would transition from one predominantly white institution to another, always aware of race and often questioning whether I belonged.

With each era that passed, I became more and more certain that I would never escape the stares. As I continually improved my life, I simultaneously moved further and further away from the world's expectations of a black man.

My early successes in life eventually started piling up high enough for others to put me on a pedestal as one that broke through adversity and clawed my way to a better life. I regularly found myself as a poster child for institutions that were eager to put me on display.

My presence being used to present an example of how underrepresented minorities not only belonged at their organization but could also thrive.

I found myself torn. On the one hand, there was immense pressure to always "bring my 'A' game." Not only was my performance a reflection of me, but also, it felt as though my successes and failures would be generalized towards the broader Black community. Grateful to have received opportunities that I never could have fathomed as a child, I wanted to keep those doors open for people who looked like me and came from communities like mine.

On the other hand, the spotlight helped amplify my voice and enabled me to give back to underrepresented minorities grappling with many of the same insecurities that I had battled earlier in life.

I decided it was time for a break. Enter Asia.

When I moved to Asia, the feeling of "all eyes on me" took a new form. My first stop was Chengdu, China. I was there long enough that I got used to the daily stares and being filmed by strangers who were not accustomed to seeing somebody black.

Race matters in the U.S. Race also matters in China. With time, I viewed the stares in China as a form of genuine curiosity. When people saw me, I certainly felt as though they were questioning what I was doing there, but I did not feel as though strangers were questioning whether I was good enough to be there.

As I got to know people better in China, my race started to matter even less. This was especially true whenever one learned of my Harvard affiliation. They did not view me as a "Black American" but rather as an "American from an elite background."

I was afforded a level of immediate respect and acceptance that never came naturally to me as a black man in America.

Fast forward a few years and I now find myself in Singapore. Race matters in the

U.S. Race matters in China. Race matters in Singapore, but has affected me less.

I landed in Singapore roughly one year ago, eager to step off the plane and into my new life. I had neither visited Singapore nor any other Southeast Asian country before.

Unlike my prior stint in Chengdu which was for a predefined period, there is no end date accompanying this move to Singapore. I arrived with an open mind and an empty canvas on which I was free to paint my life as I pleased.

Unlike my time in China, people are not staring and/or recording me as I walk around Singapore. Unlike my life in the U.S., I do not feel as though my race is a required topic of discussion when people think of me.

Despite being 10,000 miles away from where I was born, I feel more at ease with my race & identity in Singapore than I have ever felt before.

The spotlight is off, and I am free to live my life.

22.
When I Became a Food Rebel
By Elika Tasker

I know everything happens for a reason but little did I realise that Singapore was to hold my transformation to a Health Coach & Plant-Based Chef and in turn coach others through The SoulFull Program - A Transformational Program to Unleash Energy Within 30 Days!

When I moved to Singapore nine years ago, it was clear I was a foodie. I spent most weekends trying out my colleague's recommendations on the best biryani, rendang or curry puff.

My travels around the world had already introduced me to many flavours, and what I loved was to enjoy the similarities of every country's version of similar dishes. I mean, at the heart of it, a curry puff really isn't that different than a cornish pasty, empanada or Jamaican patty! Having been born in the UK with Jamaican and Costa Rican roots, spices were not new to me, so the fusion of Malay, Indian & Chinese felt amazing.

I had come to develop my corporate career at that stage. True to my black roots, I felt that the harder I worked, the more recognition I would gain. I went straight to burnout. My body could no longer take the chronic stress as a result of trying to balance all my priorities: the long hours, trying to stay fit, having a hectic social life, and nutrition that provided little support for all of the above.

I started to learn about personalised nutrition. Very quickly through this experience, I came to see my true purpose in life: educating people on how to create a healthy lifestyle with good nutrition.

Setting up my health coaching practice became the obvious path. After only one year of coaching (following 11 years in the corporate world), I then went to open Food Rebel.

This organic restaurant sat at the heart of what I wanted to share with all the wisdom of travelling worldwide & exploring different cultures cuisine: my adaptation to Asia by connecting with people through their favourite foods, to

teaching what I had taken for granted, to preparing our own food and seeing it growing in abundance around us.
Food Rebel quickly shows the community what is possible when we prepare food from scratch that is unprocessed and free of refined sugars and dairy. I wanted to be truly rebellious, to show that healthy organic food did not need to be a salad.

With the sale of the restaurant after five years last year, I've been able to support people in all aspects of their transformation through my online video training - The SoulFull Program. It's been a beautiful gift of giving back to the community where I found this opportunity and connected with my own soul. On this transformational online journey I take the individual through the fundamentals of nutrition, which involves the learning that one diet is not suitable for all & the tools to create their customised diet. We then move through working on the other aspects of their life where they are leaking energy. You see energy is pivotal to us feeling fulfilled and able to live life to the fullest. Yet so many of us carry our daily tasks with fatigue, anxiety & a body that just feels heavy. To show how to feel full vitality, love our food yet know how it aids our body as medicine and know there is another way that allows you to feel your body is thriving, has been the icing on the cake to my journey in Singapore.

23.
From Oakland to Hong Kong
By James Acey

I'm navigating my way through space and time here in 2020, by far the most interesting year of my life (our lives?). I humbly serve as a director of music here in Hong Kong.

I consider myself very lucky to have grown up in a multicultural environment. In fact, for me, relocating to Hong Kong didn't come with 'culture shock' (San Francisco's population is a fifth Chinese and overall one third Asian), but rather 'city shock'. This sprawling, dense, picturesque metropolis, which I'm still in awe of to this day, was unlike any city I'd lived in. I have enormous respect for this city's history and am grateful for the connections forged and network I've built whilst here.

The pros and cons of being anybody at all is something I often think about when assessing my journey through the various spaces I've inhabited. Being Black in America virtually forces you to become an expert on matters of race at "home" as well as your existence away from it. It is a lens that serves as a starting point for the anti-Blackness that exists all the world over, but I feel requires a filter depending on where you are.

In my experience, the lens of anti-Blackness in Hong Kong manifests itself in many forms. These forms are somewhat distinct from those in the states. Unlike America and many Western countries, it is not born out of malice, but rather ignorance and furthermore lack of interaction. There simply isn't much of a precedent for Chinese-Black relations. I do think, though, that similar to Western countries, people don't know how to interact with us. It's actually pretty simple: just treat us like human beings.

As you can clearly see with the popularity of music, fashion, and pop culture that originate from Black spaces, globally, Black identity is very culturally compelling. While many people love the products of black culture and might claim to love black people, its often the case that they *tolerate* black people to the extent that they can continue enjoying the products whilst still not truly recognizing the humanity behind the person that created their favorite dance they emulate or player that kicked the football into the net to win the game for their team.

Growing up African but very much American, in a household with my single mum's Ghanaian traditions but heavily influenced by Black American culture, sense of belonging is something that was always fleeting. Geographically, I've never felt strong feelings of 'this is the place where I belong,' yet haven't felt strong feelings to the contrary. That's not to say that I'm just comfortable anywhere, but as Gil Scott- Heron put it, '...there is no any one place where I belong, my spirit's meant to be free'. This attitude shaped my decision to relocate to Buenos Aires after university and to come to Hong Kong some ten years ago.

Settling into Hong Kong, I was never too worried about how I would be accepted. My thoughts have always been, if as a Black person, you can make it through America's racism, then you can make it anywhere. It sends you off traumatized and with emotional baggage but also somewhat battle-tested , for a battle that you never really wanted to fight no less, but without a doubt battle-tested. Sure, I've experienced many cases of racism here both overt and implicit, but it's almost a banal exercise to detail them because, one, they aren't particularly surprising, and two, at the end of the day, I've mentally and spiritually primed myself so that such encounters have as little effect on me as possible. Like many, I suppose I could probably benefit from going to therapy, but I'm using that money on piano lessons right now.

The awakening that is taking place right now in regards to Blackness is refreshing in that it is much needed, yet it is exhausting. To suddenly now have the attention of the masses for injustices you've repeatedly pointed out over decades in protest, in lyric, and in art feels very surreal and begs the question of how earnest this turn really is. I'd like to say I'm cautiously optimistic that some sort of change will come from all of this but I really don't know. Here in

Hong Kong, I don't expect these ideas to carry over in any substantial way and that's fine, respectfully the area is dealing with its own complex issues. The good thing about it all, at the very least, is the awareness to which it leads. By being present and only slightly engaged in 2020, chances are you've come across these messages and that small interaction is akin to having received the global memo.

ISBN: 978-1-7354699-0-4

Cover design by Ellie Suh (elliesuh.com)
Cover © 2020 Ellie Suh

For more information on Spill Stories, please visit instagram.com/spillstories or spillstories.club/.

To contact Tiffany Huang, the founder of Spill Stories and editor of this book, please email spillyourstories@gmail.com.

Made in the USA
Middletown, DE
02 August 2020

14340546R00080